RAIL 12 PORTFOLIOS

The 37s
Second Series

Compiled by
Paul Shannon

First published 1990

ISBN 0 7110 1931 2

© Ian Allan Ltd 1990

Published by

IAN ALLAN LTD

Terminal House Shepperton TW17 8AS
Telephone: Walton-on-Thames (0932) 228950
Fax: 0932 232366   Telex: 929806 IALLAN G
Registered Office: Terminal House Shepperton TW17 8AS
Phototypeset and Printed by Ian Allan Printing at their works at
Coombelands in Runnymede, England

Front cover:
A rare survival from the steam era was the turntable
and part roundhouse at St Blazey depot, home of BR's
Cornish china clay traction. No 37196 stands on the
turntable on 22 April 1987, just a matter of days before
the installation was taken out of service. Luckily the
roundhouse is a listed building and has been saved from
the ignoble fate of demolition. No 37196 was named
Tre Pol and Pen and painted in the first Railfreight
livery in the summer of 1985 as part of the GWR150
celebrations. Its duties as a Cornish china clay
locomotive were soon to come to an end, however, and
it was subsequently transferred to Cardiff, Inverness
and Eastfield. Its name was passed on to new arrival
No 37671 in 1987. *Les Nixon*
Pentax 6×7 105mm Takumar Ektachrome 100
1/250, f8

Introduction

Arguably the most successful of the 1955 Modernisation Plan designs, BR's Class 37 locomotives have appeared on every Region of the network and become a familiar sight to enthusiasts in all parts of the country. As befits a true mixed traffic type, these locomotives have worked almost every kind of train from express passenger to pick-up goods in their already lengthy careers. Not that these careers are drawing to a close; on the contrary the extensive refurbishment programme of the mid-1980s will ensure that some examples survive well into the next century, outliving almost all of their contemporaries from the early 1960s.

One *Rail Portfolio* has already appeared on the theme of the Class 37, so the selection of photographs which fills these pages is intended above all to show the exciting developments of the last few years. The complete internal rebuilds which resulted in sub-classes 37/4, 37/5, 37/7 and 37/9 were accompanied by external changes which make the type particularly interesting at a visual level. The removal of headcode boxes on many locomotives added a third basic variant to Class 37 front-end design, and just about every livery drawn up in the 1980s has found its way on to a Class 37: large logo, original Railfreight, 'red stripe' Railfreight, new Railfreight with sub-Sector markings, InterCity, and even 'one-offs' such as British Steel blue and original Brunswick green. Whether any Class 37 will make half a century in revenue-earning service is only open to speculation, but they will certainly remain a much valued asset to BR, especially the Railfreight Sector, for many years to come.

Thanks are due once again to the many photographers who submitted their best material for consideration for this volume.

Paul Shannon
Bolton
August 1989

Previous page:
A Class 37-hauled football special provides a welcome change from the monotony of DMUs at Seaham on the Durham coast line on 14 November 1981. The train is 1G29, the 12.41 Sunderland-Middlesbrough, and the locomotive is No 37109, based in those days at March but since reallocated to Motherwell, Inverness and Thornaby. On the left are some HTV and HTO hopper wagons awaiting loading at Seaham colliery. *Paul Shannon*
Olympus OM1 50mm Zuiko Kodachrome 64 1/250, f5.6-8

Left:
Class 37/4 No 37418 *An Comunn Gaidhealach* rests between duties at Inverness depot on 21 September 1988. This locomotive came to Inverness in January 1986 along with several other Class 37/4s to bring the comforts of electric train heating to Far North and Kyle line passenger services. It gained its name at a ceremony in Edinburgh in October 1986.
Gavin Morrison
Minolta 7000 Kodachrome 64
automatic exposure setting

Above:
The second Class 37 locomotive to receive InterCity livery was No 37409, following the example set by No 37401 in 1988. On 27 August 1989 No 37409 crosses Loch Nan Uamh Viaduct with the 'West Highlander' charter train on its Mallaig-Fort William leg. The 'Highlander' and 'West Highlander' weekend excursions from London have been a great success for InterCity, success which has justified the extensive refurbishment given to a number of Mk 1 First Open carriages in the mid-1980s. *W. A. Sharman*

3

Left:
D6736 was still very much in its youth when photographed leaving Scarborough with the 17.40 to Hull on 2 July 1965. Note the interesting rake of maroon-liveried non-corridor stock which was still in use on local services at that time. Under the Total Operations Processing System (TOPS) renumbering scheme of the 1970s this locomotive became No 37036, and in spring 1986 it assumed another new identity in the form of Class 37/5 No 37507. At the time of writing it operates from Thornaby as a member of the Railfreight Metals fleet, hauling block loads of steel from Lackenby to such places as Corby, Wolverhampton and Workington.
Barrie Walker
Super Paxette 2LT   Kodachrome II

Above:
Half a mile south of Lutterworth, on the Leicester-Rugby section of the Great Central main line, English Electric Type 3 No D6742 hurries past with the 10.08 York-Bournemouth express on 5 March 1966. By this time the English Electric (EE)-built Type 3s were appearing regularly on York-Bournemouth trains, although the Marylebone-Nottingham workings still had steam haulage. Freight traffic over this stretch of line had already ceased, and total closure was not far away. No D6742, or No 37042 as it later became, has spent most of its life as an Eastern Region machine, with just a short spell on the Western Region for crew training in the early 1960s. *Michael Mensing*
Nikkorex 'F' 50mm Nikkor f2 Agfacolor CT18 1/1000, f2

5

Above:
The train headcode 7M69 indicates a partially fitted freight to the London Midland Region, as No 6745 approaches Ancaster on the Sleaford-Grantham line with empty mineral wagons on the evening of 28 May 1966. After carrying the number 37045 for 15 years this locomotive became No 37355 in 1988, having received CP7 bogies during an earlier intermediate overhaul at Crewe Works. Since 1986 it has worked from Tinsley as a member of the Railfreight Distribution pool. *Michael Mensing Nikkorex 'F' 50mm f2 Nikkor Agfacolor CT18 1/500, f3.2*

Right:
Green livery with full yellow ends was an intermediate livery carried by many Class 37s in the early 1970s. No 6923 was in this condition when photographed climbing towards Pyle with an up South Wales main line freight on 26 May 1973. Margam steelworks is just visible on the right. No 6923 has seen less variety of train workings and settings than many of its fellow Class 37s: in summer 1989 it was still allocated to Cardiff Canton, dedicated to Speedlink Coal Network duties.
Wyn Hobson

Above:
Not yet another Railfreight livery, but just the standard works undercoat, as the last of the Class 37/4 eth conversions, No 37431, nears the end of its stay at Crewe Works on 23 March 1986. Its previous identity was No 37272, and it had spent most of its days before conversion on the Western Region, including a spell at Laira in 1983. The number 37272 was brought back into use for a different locomotive in January 1989, when No 37304 lost its original number as part of BR's plan to clear the 373XX number series of all but rebogied locomotives.
Douglas Johnson
Fujica ST605N 50mm Fujinon Agfa 100RS
1/125, f4

Right:
One of the first Class 37s to receive Railfreight Distribution livery was No 37198, seen here on the stabling point at Tyne Yard on 17 May 1989. Unlike the refurbished version below, it still carries its central headcode box which identifies it as an original Mk II variant. No 37198 is a long-standing Eastern Region locomotive, having worked from Thornaby for well over a decade before its transfer to Tinsley in 1987. *Michael Rhodes*
Mamiya 645 1000S 150mm Sekor
Ektachrome 100 1/60, f8

Right:
One of the more esoteric liveries carried by a Class 37 locomotive was British Steel blue, applied to No 37501 *Teesside Steelmaster* in February 1987. No 37501 is partnered with Railfreight-liveried sister locomotive No 37502 as it hauls 6M47, the 10.10 Lackenby-Corby steel coil train, towards Cargo Fleet on 5 January 1988. Another member of the Metals fleet, Class 37/0 No 37077, is heading in the opposite direction with a local trip working from Tees Yard to Wilton. The livery experiment on No 37501 came to an end in August 1989 when it emerged from Doncaster in standard Railfreight Metals livery. *Peter J. Robinson*
Pentax 6×7 150mm Takumar Fujichrome 400
1/500, f6.3-8

Left:
The 'large logo' livery once carried by all Class 37/4s is exemplified by this portrait of No 37425, which also sports the unforgettable 'Scottie Dog' owner-ship mark of its home depot, Eastfield. An unusual feature which defies illustration in one frame is the pair of nameplates fitted to No 37425: *Sir Robert McAlpine* on one side, and *Concrete Bob* on the other. The photograph is dated 12 June 1988, and the location is Eastfield. *Hugh Ballantyne*
Leica M3 50mm Summicron Kodachrome 25 1/60, f5.6-8

Left:
Faith in the power of television advertising led BR to adorn one of its engines in 'Police' livery for a filming session on the Newcastle-Carlisle line in July 1985. No 37093 was singled out for the most unusual task of catching up with and arresting a 'speeding' IC125 unit on the adjacent track. It is pictured outside Gateshead depot on 23 July, still minus its blue flashing light at this stage because of gauging restraints on the main line. The filming exercise did not pass without hitches: perhaps the most embarrassing was the fact that the supposedly washable white paint turned out not to be washable at all, and a trip to Stratford DRS was needed for No 37093 to have a complete repaint!
Douglas Johnson
Fujica ST605N 35mm-70mm Tamron Zoom Agfa 100RS 1/500, f5.6

One of the more pleasing livery designs applied to Class 37s was the 'red stripe' Railfreight livery. No 37002 had just been painted in this colour scheme following an overhaul when it was photographed at Crewe Works open day on 4 July 1987. No 37002 was delivered to Stratford in December 1960 and has since operated from a number of Eastern Region depots. In 1989 it became the last member of sub-Class 37/3 to receive its new identity, No 37351, and at the time of writing it works from Immingham as a member of the Railfreight Metals pool. *Chris Shaw*
Pentax LX 50mm Pentax Fujichrome 50 1/125, f8

The last nine Class 37s to roll off the production line were numbered in the D66XX series, breaking the continuity from the main series which ended at No D6999. No 6607 was delivered in October 1965, making it nearly five years younger than the oldest of its fellow class members. A long-standing Western Region locomotive, it is seen stabled between duties at Severn Tunnel Junction on 19 August 1973. In the following year it received the number 37307, and in 1984 it was one of the first Class 37s to be refurbished and fitted with eth at Crewe, emerging as No 37403. *David Rapson*
Praktica L 50mm Praktica Agfa CT18 1/125, f8

Above:
Crossing the ill-fated bridge over the River Ness at Inverness on 22 February 1986 is Class 37/4 No 37417, hauling the 11.35 to Wick and Thurso. After the bridge collapsed in the severe flooding of 7 February 1989, No 37417 was one of six Class 37s marooned on the 'wrong' side and spent rather longer than it had anticipated away from its home depot, Inverness. It received its name *Highland Region* upon transfer to Inverness at the end of 1985, having spent the previous 12 months based at Eastfield and many years prior to that in South Wales. *Jeremy Hunns*
Canon AE-1 50mm Canon Kodachrome 64 1/250, f4-5.6

Right:
No 37114 *Dunrobin Castle* skirts Loch Carron between Stromeferry and Attadale on 18 June 1988 with the 'Royal Scotsman' luxury tour train from Kyle of Lochalsh. It would remain in charge of the train as far as Inverness. New to Tinsley in 1963, No 37114 was transferred to the Scottish Region in 1981 and became one of the replacements for Class 26 traction on the Kyle and Far North lines in the following year. Since it has no eth capability it is more usually seen on freight duties these days, although summer passenger workings pose no real difficulties. *Hugh Ballantyne*
Leica M3 50mm Summicron Kodachrome 25 1/500, f2-2.8

Left:
Sun and snow do not often occur together, but the snow-capped tops of Clach Leathad provide a fine setting for No 37404 as it rounds the curve near Achallader on the long climb from Bridge of Orchy to Rannoch on 9 April 1988. The train is the 09.50 Glasgow Queen Street-Fort William. No 37404 was formerly South Wales locomotive No 37286, but its new allegiance to Scotland was confirmed in 1986 when it received the name *Ben Cruachan* at a ceremony in Oban. *Les Nixon*

Pentax 6×7 105mm Takumar Fujichrome 100 1/500, f5.6

Above:
At a time when any variation from standard rail blue livery was officially frowned upon by BR, Eastfield depot was brave enough to apply wrap-around yellow ends to three of its Class 37s used on West Highland line services. No 37112, a temporary carrier of this non-standard colour scheme, propels a rake of Mk 1 stock into Mallaig station on the morning of 27 August 1981, ready to form the next departure to Fort William. On the right are fuel oil tanks for the local fishing industry which would have been brought to Mallaig on the back of an earlier passenger service. This unusual practice of mixed train working continued on the Mallaig line into the late 1980s, long after it had been abandoned elsewhere. *Paul Shannon*
Olympus OM1 50mm Zuiko Kodachrome 64 1/250, f6-8

Left:
Against the massive backdrop of the Grampian mountains, with peaks rising to over 2,500ft, the 18.10 Fort William-London Euston sleeper train climbs from the Horseshoe Curve towards County March summit near Tyndrum on 15 June 1988. At this time the train still carried a seating portion from Mallaig to Glasgow, but with the arrival of Sprinter units in January 1989 the sleeper train became a self-contained working with its departure time from Fort William delayed by 2hr. The locomotive is Class 37/4 No 37403 *Isle of Mull*, formerly No 37307 and before that D6607 as illustrated on page 11.

Hugh Ballantyne
Leica M3 90mm Summicron Kodachrome 25
1/250, f4

Above:
No 37423 was the first Class 37/4 to receive Railfreight livery, complete with Metals sub-Sector logos. It was named after Sir Murray Morrison, pioneer of the British aluminium industry, at a ceremony in Fort William in May 1988. Traffic to and from the Lochaber works at Fort William forms an important part of freight carryings on the West Highland line, including the block trains of alumina which run most days from Blyth in Northeast England. Traction resources are commonly shared between business Sectors in BR's remoter regions, however, and this explains the appearance of No 37423 on one of Britain's most prestigious private touring trains, the 'Royal Highlander', on 14 June 1988. The train is pictured shortly after leaving Crianlarich on its way to Oban.
Hugh Ballantyne
Leica M3 50mm Summicron Kodachrome 25
1/500, f2.8

17

Above:
No 37431 *Sir Powys – County of Powys* climbs towards Dorrington, between Shrewsbury and Church Stretton with the 09.15 Liverpool Lime Street-Cardiff Central service on 6 May 1989. This working was one of several which had temporarily been restored to locomotive haulage after the withdrawal of the Class 155 Sprinters for fault rectification in December 1988. No 37431 was the last of the eth-fitted sub-class to emerge from Crewe Works back in April 1986. *Wyn Hobson*
Pentax Spotmatic II 55mm Takumar
Kodachrome 64 1/500, f4-5.6

Right:
By the start of the summer 1989 timetable the Class 155 fleet had still not been fully restored to service, and Class 37/4s continued to make regular appearances over the North & West route. No 37427 pulls away from Craven Arms with the 05.07 Cardiff Central-Liverpool Lime Street service on 27 May. This locomotive was named *Bont y Bermo* at Barmouth in 1986 to celebrate the return of locomotive-hauled trains to the Cambrian Coast line. *Don Gatehouse*
Nikon FE 85mm Nikkor Kodachrome 64
1/500, f4

Left:
Class 37/4 No 37429 approaches Shrewsbury on 19 April 1989 with the 07.14 Aberystwyth-London Euston service. Despite the air-conditioned Inter-City rolling stock this train is sponsored by the Provincial Sector for the section of its journey west of Shrewsbury. If InterCity were to sponsor the train throughout, it would have to pay a proportion of the fixed costs of the Cambrian line, which as a financially self-supporting organisation it would not want to do. The 'Cambrian Coast Express' headboard serves to remind present-day travellers of a bygone age long before the idea of business

Sectors became a reality. No 37429 has carried two names in its relatively short career as an eth locomotive: first it was named *Sir Dyfed – County of Dyfed* in April 1986, and then it was renamed *Eisteddfod Genedlaethol* in August of the same year. *Brian Denton*
Nikkormat 85mm Nikon Kodachrome 25 1/500, f2.8

Above:
Locomotive-hauled trains returned to the Cambrian Coast line in April 1986 after a gap of nearly five years. During this time the Class 25s which used to

operate freight workings on the line had become virtually extinct, and the new through passenger services between Pwllheli and London were inaugurated with Class 37/4 motive power. During the second summer of the Cambrian Coast renaissance, on 26 September 1987, Nos 37429 and 37426 pass between lower and upper quadrant semaphores as they approach Sutton Bridge Junction, just south of Shrewsbury, with the 07.40 Euston-Pwllheli service. *Hugh Ballantyne*
Leica M3 50mm Summicron Kodachrome 25 1/500, f2.8

Left:
The North Wales Coast line was used to test refurbished Class 37s as they were outshopped from Crewe Works, sometimes on special test trains and sometimes at the head of timetabled passenger services. Class 37/5 No 37678 leads Class 47 No 47603 *County of Somerset* towards Prestatyn with the 11.16 Crewe-Holyhead service on 6 May 1987. No 37678 was renumbered from No 37256 during its stay at Crewe Works, and since its refurbishment it has worked from Tinsley as a member of the Buxton Stone pool. *David Rapson*

Canon AE-1 50mm Canon Kodachrome 64 1/500, f5-5.6

Above:
For many years D6700's honour as the first-built member of its class was masked by an irregularity in the 1973 TOPS renumbering scheme. No locomotive was to carry a number ending in '000', so instead of becoming No 37000, D6700 was tacked on to the end of the number series allotted to Mk 1 Class 37s and given the number 37119. In 1988, however, it found itself at the beginning of a

number series again, this time as No 37350, since it had been fitted with CP7 bogies and reclassified '37/3'. The former D6700 claimed further distinction when it was repainted in original green livery, albeit with full yellow ends, and it has rapidly become a sought-after hauler of railtours and service trains alike. It is seen passing under the gaze of at least two photographers near Dorrington with the 07.03 Cardiff-Liverpool on 27 May 1989.
Wyn Hobson
Pentax Spotmatic II 135mm Tamron Kodachrome 64 1/500, f4-5.6

23

Above:
Class 37/4 locomotives Nos 37427 and 37426 await departure from Crewe station with the 00.42 Manchester Piccadilly-Cardiff on 2 June 1986. This was a Mondays-only working which conveyed passengers and parcels; on other days of the week it was replaced by an 02.04 Crewe-Cardiff which conveyed TPO traffic additionally. The twin Class 37/4 haulage was a means of returning locomotives to their home depot at Canton after working Cambrian passenger services on the Saturday. From May 1989 the train ceased to appear in the passenger timetable but continued to run for parcels traffic. The pairing of Nos 37427 and 37426 is significant since these two machines were the first to cross the revitalised Barmouth Bridge upon reopening to locomotive-hauled trains in April 1986. *David Rapson*
Canon AE-1 50mm Canon Kodachrome 64 6sec, f5.6

Right:
Freight trains rarely stop in the right place to enable night photography to be carried out, but an exception was made on 9 November 1985 (at the unearthly hour of 04.20!) when No 37107 paused at Newcastle Central station with a southbound train of petroleum tanks. No 37107 left its native Eastern Region in May 1987 and spent a few months based at Motherwell and Eastfield, but by November it was back at Stratford where it became a member of the Freightliner pool. In July 1989 maintenance responsibility for this pool was transferred from Stratford to Tinsley. *Chris Shaw*
Pentax ME Super 50mm Pentax Kodachrome 64 30sec, f4.5

Above:
One of the first locomotive pools to be fully dedicated to a specific traffic flow was the North Thameside Petroleum pool, comprising approximately 10 Class 37/7s based at Stratford. These locomotives were amongst the first to carry Railfreight Petroleum livery. Class 37/7 No 37891, renumbered from Class 37/0 No 37166, passes Kensal Green Junction on 31 October 1988 with 6V33, the 13.45 Ripple Lane-Thame oil train. The tanks had been loaded at one of the refineries at Thames Haven and brought to Ripple Lane yard by

a separate trip working earlier in the day.
Paul Shannon
Olympus OM1 135mm Zuiko Kodachrome 64 1/250, f4-5.6

Right:
Freight traffic over the Standedge route declined dramatically after the reopening of the more gently graded Calder Valley line in August 1985. One service which has continued to use the Standedge route, however, is the daily tank train from Haverton Hill to Glazebrook and back. It is

virtually forced to use this route since there is no convenient connection in Manchester between the Calder Valley line and the ex-CLC line through Glazebrook. Another interesting feature of this train is the regular use of a Railfreight Metals Class 37/5 on a Petroleum sub-Sector service. No 37519 was in charge on 1 April 1989, and is seen passing Stalybridge with 6E20, the 10.08 empties from Glazebrook to Haverton Hill. *Paul Shannon*
Olympus OM1 135mm Zuiko Kodachrome 64 1/250, f5.6

Above:
Tinsley-based Class 37/5s are used mainly in pairs on limestone trains from Tunstead and Peak Forest. A single example may often be seen, however, on local trip workings between Peak Forest sidings and the freight terminals at Hope (Blue Circle Cement) and Hindlow (Steetley). No 37679 approaches Edale on 17 August 1988 with empty cement tanks for Hope, running as trip T82 from Peak Forest. The diagram will continue with No 37679 bringing loaded tanks to Peak Forest and then visiting Hindlow to exchange empty lime wagons for loaded ones. Having returned to Peak Forest for the second time it will then haul the afternoon Speedlink feeder service to Northenden and Warrington. *Paul Shannon*
Olympus OM1 135mm Zuiko Kodachrome 64 1/250, f5.6

Right:
Class 37/5 No 37511 ambles down the Wear Valley near Frosterley with 6N31, the 18.30 Eastgate-Tyne Yard cement train, on 7 June 1988. From Tyne Yard the tanks will be despatched to various destinations by scheduled Speedlink services. No 37511 was converted from No 37103 in 1986 and subsequently allocated to the Railfreight Metals pool based at Thornaby. It was named *Stockton Haulage* after the road haulier of that name who broke new ground by using Railfreight to transport his consignments of steel from Teesside to a specially-built terminal at Stranraer.
Peter J. Robinson
Pentax 6×7 150mm Takumar Fujichrome 400 1/500, f9

Left:
Class 37/5 locomotives Nos 37510 and 37513 pass Clay Cross with a uniform load of emtpy BBA steel carriers on the evening of 29 June 1989. The train is 6E82, the 15.16 return service from Wolverhampton Steel Terminal to BSC Lackenby. Both locomotives carry the earlier Railfreight livery, but have larger-than-standard bodyside numbers similar to those applied to Class 37/4s. Before refurbishment they were Nos 37112 (see also page 15) and 37056 respectively. *Paul Shannon*

Olympus OM1   100mm Zuiko   Kodachrome 64   1/500, f4

Above:
Cardiff Class 37s took over from paired Class 20s on the Dee Marsh-Warrington leg of Dee Marsh-Mossend steel trains in January 1989. No 37710, painted in new Railfreight Metals livery, passes Helsby on Saturday 17 June 1989 with 6S42, the 08.20 from Dee Marsh to Mossend. Normally these trains comprise just empty steel coil carriers but on this occasion the load included nine Tiger POA wagons carrying scrap from BSC Shotton to BSC Clydesdale. After arrival at Warrington Bank Quay, 6S42 would have been taken forward by electric traction and No 37710 would have waited for the next loaded train for Dee Marsh.
Paul Shannon
Olympus OM1   100mm Zuiko   Kodachrome 64   1/500, f4-5.6

31

Left:

From humble beginnings in the mid-1970s rail traffic from Boulby mine has grown considerably in recent years and attracted the use of a wide variety of wagon types. The motive power has seen some variation, too, with Classes 20, 31, 37 and 47 all making regular trips along the single-track branch from Skinningrove. A Thornaby-based Class 37/5 locomotive, No 37503, was in charge of the morning trip working from Boulby to Middlesbrough on 11 March 1987, and is pictured crossing over on to the main line at South Bank. This locomotive had yet to acquire its name *British Steel Shelton* which was transferred from unrefurbished sister locomotive No 37077 in July of the same year.
Peter J. Robinson
Pentax 6×7 150mm Takumar Ektachrome 200 1/500, f8

Above:

No 37051 approaches Heaton with 6S54, the 09.05 Thrislington-Ravenscraig dolophines train, on 28 April 1989. This train has caused a great deal of controversy because of the shower of lime which falls as it passes. One lady claimed that whilst she stood on Berwick station the train wrought irreparable damage to her fur coat and tried to sue BR for a new garment! Attempts to cover the fine chippings with a protective coat were unsuccessful and the train continues to provide a most dramatic sight when travelling at high speed.
Michael Rhodes
Mamiya 645 1000S 150mm Sekor Ektachrome 100 1/250, f5.6-8

Above:
Many readers will remember the triple-headed Class 37s which used to haul BR's heaviest trains carrying iron ore from Port Talbot to Llanwern. After a spell with paired Class 56 haulage these trains were handed back to Class 37s during 1988, but this time without the need for triple-headers: it was found that just two of the refurbished and ballasted Class 37/7s or 37/9s were equal to the task performed by three of their predecessors. The two named Class 37/9s, Nos 37905 *Vulcan Enterprise* and 37901 *Mirrlees Pioneer* are seen passing Ebbw Junction and Alexandra Dock Junction with an

evening train of empties to Port Talbot on 23 June 1989. By this time the other four Class 37/9s had been repainted in new-style Railfreight Metals livery, but Nos 37901 and 37905 were still carrying the older Railfreight colour scheme. *Geoff Cann Pentax 6×7 Fujichrome 100 1/500, f4*

Right:
Class 37/7 No 37714 takes 6V99, the 14.53 Hamworthy-Cardiff Tidal steel train, along the Wylye valley near Norton Bavant on 23 May 1989. The formation comprises two Powell Duffryn PXA coil wagons and three BDA bogie bolsters. This

train exists primarily for imported steel traffic from Hamworthy Docks to South Wales, the West Midlands and Swindon. In line with BR's policy of sub-Sector dedication the train has been diagrammed for a Metals Class 37 instead of a Speedlink Class 47 since May 1989. Two months later it was diverted away from the Wylye valley route in order to serve Swindon en route to Cardiff, rather than having the Swindon traffic conveyed by a connecting service from Cardiff. *Steve McMullin Minolta X700 50mm Minolta Kodachrome 64 1/500, f4*

Above:
Steel coil is conveyed to Shotton (Dee Marsh Junction) both from South Wales and from Ravenscraig, but after discharge most of the wagons return empty to Ravenscraig, since there is also a flow of coil from Ravenscraig to South Wales. This ensures maximum wagon utilisation. An exception to the scheme, however, is train number 6V42, which runs on Saturday mornings and conveys empties direct from Dee Marsh Junction to Margam. This train is illustrated approaching Craven Arms on 25 June 1988, with motive power provided by blue-liveried Class 37/0 No 37275 in place of the more usual refurbished machine.
Don Gatehouse
Nikon FE 235mm Nikkor Kodachrome 64 1/500, f4

Right:
Class 37/7 No 37711 *Tremorfa Steelworks* heads into a rainstorm near Nantwich on 12 January 1989 with 6V75, the 06.35 Mossend-Cardiff Tidal steel coil train. This train conveys traffic from the British Steel rolling mill at Ravenscraig to the tinplate works at Ebbw Vale, Trostre and Velindre. No 37711 entered traffic in June 1988 after refurbishment at Crewe Works, having previously been No 37085. *David Rapson*
Canon AE-1 50mm Canon Kodachrome 64 1/500, f4

Above:
Situated high up above the Taff and Rhymney valleys, at the end of a 10-mile freight-only line, Cwmbargoed has become one of the busier locations for despatching coal traffic in South Wales. It is not unusual for trains to run there at weekends, and on Saturday 14 January 1989 Class 37/7 No 37798 is seen arriving at Cwmbargoed with 6C86, the 09.10 merry-go-round (MGR) empties from Aberthaw power station. No 37798 was renumbered from Class 37/0 No 37006 in 1986 and had been based at several Eastern Region depots before its conversion. It was unusual in losing its headcode boxes before its refurbishment – a consequence of collision damage.
Don Gatehouse
Nikon FE 85mm Nikkor Kodachrome 64 1/500, f4

Right:
Some of the heaviest MGR trains running on BR are those which convey imported coal from Hunterston to Ravenscraig. The standard train length is 46 HAAs. Traction resources for these trains are shared with those used on Hunterston-Ravenscraig iron ore trains and comprise (at the time of writing) 17 Class 37s based at Motherwell. An evening trainload of coal approaches West Kilbride station on 4 April 1989, with traction provided by Class 37/0s Nos 37092 and 37049. The latter locomotive had recently received Railfreight Metals livery whilst its partner retained rail blue. An ususual feature of the Largs branch is that only one track is electrified between Ardrossan and Hunterston, so that the former 'up' or Glasgow-bound track is effectively freight only.
Paul Shannon
Olympus OM1 135mm Zuiko Kodachrome 64 1/250, f5.6

Left:
Unfitted coal trains continued to run in South Wales until 1987 when the outmoded shipment facilities at Swansea were finally replaced by a more modern system. The now-closed Aberpergwm branch is the setting for Class 37/0 No 37222 as it passes near the tiny settlement of Clyne with a mixture of MCV, MDV, HTV and MDO wagons on 16 April 1982, running as 9B84 Aberpergwm-Swansea Eastern Docks. No 37222 has spent much of its life working coal trains in the Welsh valleys, and was allotted to the Speedlink Coal Network, still based at Cardiff,

when BR's traction resources were officially shared out between sub-Sectors.
Paul Shannon
Olympus OM1 50mm Zuiko Kodachrome 64 1/500, f4-5.6

Above:
The use of train headcodes on BR was officially discontinued in 1976, after which most headcode boxes were fixed at the setting '0O00'. This is the code almost displayed by Class 37 No 37270 as it heads an empty mineral train through the closed

station at Sutton Park on 2 June 1977. The blue livery would at that stage have been carried by all 308 Class 37s, a far cry from the situation in the 1990s! The line through Sutton Park has remained busy with freight traffic long after its closure to passengers, since it provides a convenient link between Bescot yard and the former Midland Railway line through Washwood Heath.
Michael Mensing
Bronica S2A 75mm Nikkor
Agfachrome 50S rated at 160ASA 1/1000, f5

Left:
Class 37/0 No 37306 enters Radyr yard with the 6C73 service from Abercwmboi to Severn Tunnel Junction on 3 July 1986. Abercwmboi is the name given to the BR location which serves Aberaman phurnacite works and fuel is despatched from there to just about every coal depot in the country. The large marshalling yard at Severn Tunnel Junction is now nothing more than a memory, but Radyr has continued to play a major role in the Speedlink Coal Network, acting as a collecting point for traffic from Aberaman, Deep Navigation, Onllwyn, Gwaun-cae-Gurwen and Coedbach. *Michael Rhodes*
Canon AE-1 5mm Canon Kodachrome 64
1/250, f5.6

Above:
Smartly repainted in Railfreight Coal livery, Class 37/5 No 37698 sets off from Tondu with the 6B68 MGR service from Maesteg to Abercwmboi on 28 April 1989. The coal would be used as a raw material at Aberaman phurnacite works. The branches from Tondu to Raglan, Garw and Wyndham were all closed in the 1980s, but Maesteg has continued to produce traffic for several locations including Abercwmboi, Newport Docks and Cardiff. No 37698 was one of the very first Class 37/5 conversions, released from works in February 1986. It gained the name *Coedbach* in September 1988 upon the commissioning of new facilities at Coedbach washery. *Geoff Cann*
Pentax MX 50mm Pentax Kodachrome 64
1/250, f5.6

Left:
The engineers' sidings at Bristol East provide a busy setting for No 37425 as it heads east with 6C34, the 10.40 Radyr-Exmouth Junction Speedlink Coal Network (SCN) service, on 13 March 1989. No 37425 was one of several eth-fitted Class 37/4s displaced from Inverness in January 1989 when Sprinter DMUs took over passenger services to Kyle, Wick and Thurso. It was reallocated first to Cardiff as a member of the Mendip Stone pool and then, in May 1989, to Tinsley for use on Buxton area stone trains. The SCN working to Exmouth Junction has had an equally varied history: it was rerouted via Westbury and Yeovil in January 1988 to serve a new coal depot at Yeovil Junction, and 12

months later the starting point was amended to Radyr instead of Washwood Heath. *Geoff Cann Pentax MX 105mm Pentax Kodachrome 64 1/500, f4*

Above:
Neasden coal concentration depot is one of the last survivors of its kind in the London area. By summer 1989 the only others still operative were at West Drayton, Bow and Purley. It is reached by a spur from the freight-only Brent-Acton line, linking up with the suburban passenger line from Marylebone. Railfreight Coal-liveried Class 37/0 No 37167 propels loaded HEAs into the depot on 3 July 1989, having just arrived with 6V01 06.35 Southall-

Neasden SCN service. After positioning the loaded wagons No 37167 will return to Southall with the empties as 6A38, the 09.30 departure. Headcode experts may notice an oddity here in that 'V' denotes an inter-regional train but 'A' a train staying within the same region! The explanation is that the outward train runs via Acton Wells Junction (LMR) but the return working is booked over Western Region metals via West Ruislip, even though the latter route is rarely used in practice.
Paul Shannon
Olympus OM1 50mm Zuiko Kodachrome 64 1/250, f5.6

Above:
No 37165 stands in the exchange sidings at Maerdy on 7 July 1986. The last coal came to the surface during this week and the BR branch finally closed in October 1986 after the 30,000 tonnes of coal lying on the surface at Maerdy had been washed and despatched. This service is the 7C70 trip from Radyr which ran from Radyr to Maerdy and then to Abercwmboi phurnacite plant before returning to Radyr with empty wagons. Coal from Maerdy pit is now brought to the surface at Tower colliery on the other side of the mountain, which makes the rail journey to Abercwmboi considerably easier.
Michael Rhodes
Canon AE-1 135mm Canon Kodachrome 64 1/250, f5.6

Right:
No 37239 departs from the coke works at Nantgarw on 22 January 1985. Its load comprises a rake of ZAV departmental tube wagons and empty MDV mineral wagons. During the year-long miners' strike very little coal was carried on BR, but by January 1985 BR began to anticipate an end to the dispute and set about restoring its vast fleet of coal-carrying wagons to serviceable condition. This trip from Radyr was a special working to pick up MDV wagons for inspection and maintenance at Radyr yard. The coke works at Nantgarw was to close a year later. *Michael Rhodes*
Canon AE-1 200mm Canon Kodachrome 64 1/250, f5.6

Left:
The Speedlink Coal Network was established in 1986-87 in an attempt to tidy up the distribution of household coal and make the Railfreight Coal sub-Sector more directly accountable for this side of its operations. A number of SCN services were short-lived because there was simply not enough traffic on offer, but amongst the more successful services were those linking the coal-producing areas of England and Wales with receiving depots in the Scottish lowlands. For a time there were even Sunday workings direct from Grimethorpe Coalite plant to Mossend, and one such train is pictured near Lamberton behind No 37013 on 5 July 1987. This locomotive was pencilled in as a Class 37/5 conversion at one stage, but its refurbishment was cancelled and it became one of the last Class 37s to emerge from Crewe Works in blue livery. Note, however, the distinctive white stripe.
Peter J. Robinson
Pentax 6×7 150mm Takumar Ektachrome 200 1/1000, f4

Above:
No 37193 heads the 10.20 Didcot-Chessington South SCN service near Moreton on 12 February 1988. Later in the same year Chessington coal depot closed to rail traffic, but Didcot continued in its role as a collecting point for domestic coal traffic bound for the Southeast. Maybe if all Chessington trains had been as well loaded as this one the service would still be running today! *Brian Denton*
Mamiya 645 1000S 150mm Mamiya EPN 100 1/500, f5.6

Above:
Class 37/5 locomotives Nos 37684 and 37682 tackle the incline from Manchester Victoria to Collyhurst Street with an extra Saturday working of empties from Salford Hope Street to Peak Forest on 6 May 1989. The wagons are mostly orange-liveried PHAs belonging to RMC which were originally built for the Washwood Heath flow. No 37684 is painted in new Railfreight livery but still without sub-Sector logos, a fairly common occurrence during 1989. The two locomotives pictured here were formerly Nos 37134 and 37236 respectively. *Paul Shannon Olympus OM1 100mm Zuiko Kodachrome 64 1/250, f5.6-8*

Right:
Rounding the curve at Peak Forest on the afternoon of 29 June 1989 are Class 37/5 locomotives Nos 37683 and 37685, in charge of the 7H18 Dean Lane-Tunstead empties. This service is one of several which rely on ICI's fleet of vacuum-braked bogie hopper wagons (code PHV), some of which date back to the 1930s. Other destinations regularly served by trainloads of PHVs from Tunstead include Collyhurst Street (Manchester), Bredbury, Lostock (Northwich), Oakleigh and Hindlow. The 1990s should see the pairs of Class 37 locomotives on these services gradually replaced by single Class 60s, but there are no known plans to replace the PHV wagons at the time of writing.
Paul Shannon
Olympus OM1 50mm Zuiko Kodachrome 64 1/500, f4-5.6

Left:
Nos 37256 and 37305 head the 14.15 Westbury-Merehead trip along the Merehead branch on 29 July 1982. The train is conveying empty MSVs for loading at the Foster Yeoman quarry and eventual despatch to one of the company's London area terminals. The days of low capacity vacuum-braked wagons such as these were already numbered and soon all revenue-earning services out of Merehead would operate with more modern stock. No 37256 was of a batch then allocated to Bristol for Westbury stone traffic but since replaced in turn by Class 56s and Class 59s. It later became No 37678 and is illustrated as such on page 22. No 37305 underwent conversion, too, but this was for it to become an eth-fitted machine, No 37407.
Paul Shannon
Olympus OM1 50mm Zuiko Kodachrome 64 1/500, f5.6

Above:
Under full-scale Sectorisation it is unusual to find one sub-Sector's locomotives working another sub-Sector's trains. Especially so in the case of Stratford's Railfreight Petroleum fleet, which even has a specific link of drivers allotted to it. A rare sighting, therefore, was that of Class 37/7 No 37708 near Syston with a northbound train of empty MSV stone wagons on 13 April 1988. *Brian Denton Nikkormat 105mm Nikon Kodachrome 25 1/500, f2.8*

53

Left:
One of the most extensive colliery railway systems to survive into the 1980s was the one at Ashington, latterly operated by a small fleet of ex-BR Class 14 locomotives. On 30 October 1985, Class 37 No 37076 arrives at Ashington with a brake van in order to collect a trainload of coal for Blyth. The brake van was necessary because at this time unfitted HUO wagons were still being used on local workings. The last BR train left Ashington in December 1986 and the internal traffic ceased shortly afterwards. Now the railway system has been almost completely dismantled, leaving just one running line to the opencast disposal point at Butterwell. *Paul Shannon*
Olympus OM1 50mm Zuiko Kodachrome 64 1/250, f4-5.6

Above:
No 37087 sets back into Temple Mills yard on 4 July 1989 after an unsuccessful attempt to depart with the 07.08 Speedlink trip to Stratford Market. It will have to await the arrival of an incoming train before gaining access to the main line. The load comprises 10 TTA tanks with sulphuric acid from Avonmouth. Lurking in the background is another Class 37, No 37893, waiting to take a Speedlink trip to Bow. Despite the unrelenting rationalisation of Railfreight infrastructure and the closure of so many sidings and yards, a continued role has been identified for Temple Mills as a collecting point for freight to and from East London, and the main access lines to the yard were electrified during 1988. *Paul Shannon*
Olympus OM1 50mm Zuiko Kodachrome 64 1/250, f5.6

Right:
Not much room for manoeuvre left for No 37226, photographed at Manors on permanent way duty on 17 April 1988. This locomotive left the Eastern Region in January 1988 and was officially a Western Region locomotive at the time of the photograph. It was reallocated to Motherwell in the following month, May 1988, and renumbered 37379 to acknowledge the fact that it has CP7 bogies.
Peter J. Robinson
Pentax 6×7 150mm Takumar
Fujichrome 400 1/125, f16

Left:
Tinsley has become the home depot for virtually all BR's traction used on Speedlink services. The pool consists largely of Class 47s but includes a number of Class 31s and Class 37s for less demanding duties. Tinsley-allocated Class 37/0 No 37251 passes Moore, just south of Warrington, with a Speedlink feeder service from Warrington to Ellesmere Port on the evening of 16 May 1989. The train is conveying a mixture of empty chemical tanks for Associated Octel and empty bitumen tanks for Shell, plus the obligatory VDA barrier wagons and and brake van for this type of traffic.
Paul Shannon
Olympus OM1 50mm Zuiko Kodachrome 64 1/500, f4-5.6

Above:
The first Class 37 to receive Railfreight Distribution livery was No 37673. It was unveiled with its new coat of paint at Stratford in September 1987. Since its conversion to a Class 37/5 it worked from Laira as a member of the Cornish china clay pool, and it is seen approaching Lostwithiel with a trainload of CDAs from Moorswater on 17 February 1988. The wagons will be left at Lostwithiel for transfer to Fowey by a different locomotive. This was the first week that all china clay trains had been operated by air-braked CDAs, having finally ousted their vacuum-braked predecessors, the OOVs or 'clay hoods'. *Paul Shannon*
Olympus OM1 50mm Zuiko Kodachrome 64 1/500, f4-5.6

Left:

No 37299 approaches Coombe Junction with the morning consignment of china clay from Moorswater dries on 12 July 1980. The train is formed of traditional 'clay hood' wagons. At this time Class 37 motive power was something of a rarity in the Southwest, with many clay trains still handled by Class 25s. Since this photograph was taken No 37299 has been based at numerous depots in different parts of the country: it went from Laira to Landore in October 1982, then to Bristol Bath Road, Motherwell, Eastfield, Landore (again),

Eastfield (again) and finally to Cardiff. It was converted to a Class 37/4 towards the end of the Crewe refurbishment programme and emerged with the number 37426, subsequently to be named *Y Lein Fach/Vale of Rheidol*. *Paul Shannon*
Olympus OM1 75mm-150mm Zuiko zoom Kodachrome 64 1/250, f5.6-8

Above:

The tranquil flavour of the Fowey branch is encapsulated in this view of No 37672 *Freight Transport Association* heading towards Lostwithiel

on 29 July 1988. Up to eight trips may be made each weekday from Lostwithiel to Fowey and back, conveying china clay from various inland locations to the ECC shipment terminal at Carne Point. Many of the Cornish china clay trains cover very short distances by today's standards, and it is pleasing that Railfreight has managed to fight off competition from road hauliers and retain its involvement with this staple Cornish commodity
Hugh Ballantyne
Leica M3 50mm Summicron Kodachrome 25 1/250, f4

Left:
Despite the ac electrification of the North London line in 1988, a number of Freightliner services between Anglia and London Midland regions have continued to run with paired Class 37 haulage. Passing Highbury & Islington on 3 July 1989 are Nos 37218 and 37194, in charge of 4M54, the 14.20 Stratford-Willesden service. Although No 37194 is wearing the 'correct' Railfreight Distribution livery for a Freightliner service, its blue-liveried sister No 37218 was officially a member of the Stratford

aggregates pool at the time of this photograph.
Paul Shannon
Olympus OM1 50mm Zuiko Kodachrome 64 1/500, f4-5.6

Above:
The Felixstowe branch is one which has seen a steady increase in traffic over the last few years, this being a reflection of the growth in deep-sea container traffic handled at Felixstowe. In 1989 most trains on the branch were handled by single

Class 47s or paired Class 37s, usually with a locomotive change at Ipswich Yard. Nos 37059 *Port of Tilbury* and 37019 display their Railfreight Distribution livery to good effect as they coast round the curve towards Ipswich Yard on 11 July 1989. The train is 4E50, the 18.27 Felixstowe North-Leeds. *Paul Shannon*
Olympus OM1 100mm Zuiko Kodachrome 64 1/250, f4-5.6

Above:
Memories of Cambridge with semaphores . . . No 37087 stands at the head of a breakdown train in the yard adjacent to the station on 12 November 1980. In the background are a rake of HTV hopper wagons from the Fen Drayton-King's Cross circuit and a number of chemical tanks from Ciba-Geigy at Duxford. Class 37s were a common sight on passenger trains at Cambridge until ousted by Class 47s in May 1983, but remain part of the East

Anglian scene on freight workings to the presentday. *Paul Shannon*
Olympus OM1 75mm-150mm Zuiko zoom
Kodachrome 64 1/250, f5.6

Back cover:
Rounding the curve at Buxworth, between Chinley and New Mills, are Class 37/5 locomotives Nos 37687 and 37688, heading the 14.59 Peak Forest-Hope Street stone train (code 6J46) on

29 June 1989. The train includes a number of Tiphook bogie hoppers which had only recentlystarted operating in the Buxton area. Both locomotives look smart in the full version of Railfreight Construction livery, and No 37688 carries the name *Great Rocks* which it acquired at a ceremony marking the new flow of stone to Hindlow in June 1988. *Paul Shannon*
Olympus OM1 100mm Zuiko Kodachrome 64 1/500, f4-5.6